LET'S-READ-AND-FIND-OUT BOOK CLUB ED

ALL AROUND YOU

by FRANKLYN M. BRANLEY
illustrated by ROBERT GALSTER

THOMAS Y. CROWELL COMPANY · NEW YORK

A house full.
A barn full.
You can't get a spoonful.

What is it?

You guessed right.
It is AIR.

Air is all around you.
It is around your house.
It is around your school.
Air is all around everything.

Air is in things, too.

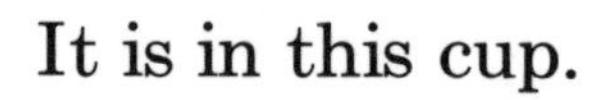

It is in this cup.

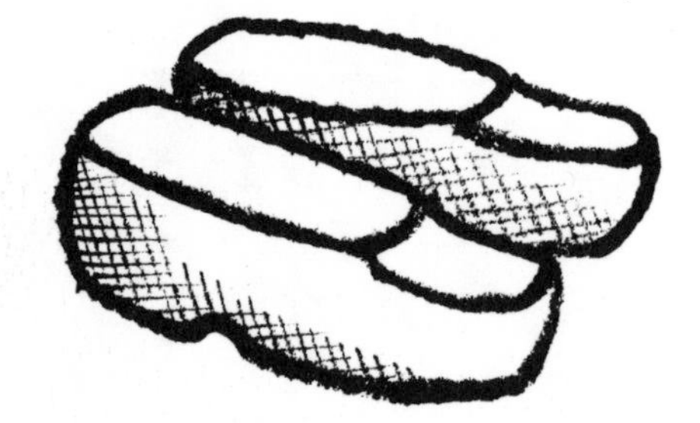

It is in your rubbers.

It is in this desk.

It is in this room.

It is even in things that look empty.

Here is a glass.

There is no water in it.

There is no milk in it.

There is no soda in it.

The glass looks empty,

but it is not.

The glass is full of air,

and you can prove it.

Fill the kitchen sink half full of water.
Color the water with blueing.
Do not use much—
just enough to color the water a little.
Put a paper napkin into a glass.
Stuff the paper in tightly so it will not fall out.
Turn the glass upside down.

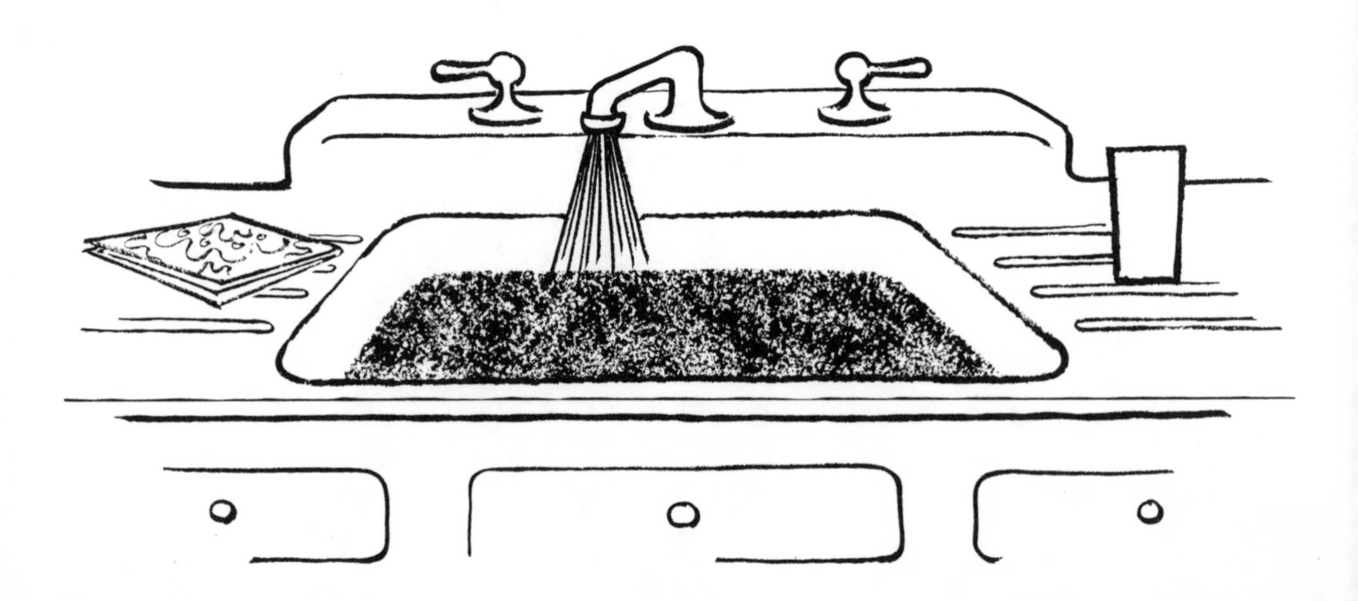

Hold the glass with two hands.
Hold it straight up and down.
Do not tip it.

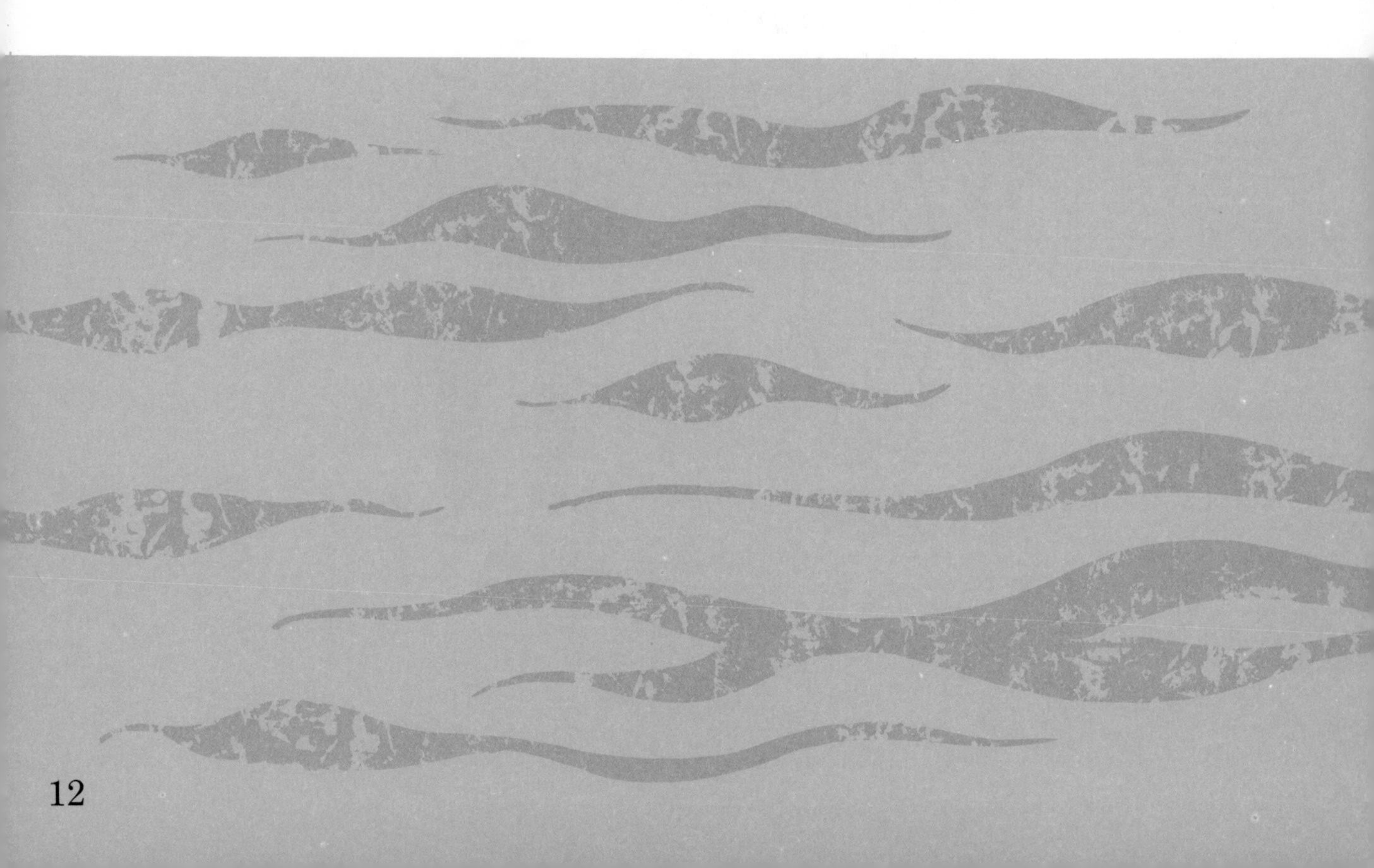

Push the glass all the way under the water.
Be sure to keep it upside down.

Pull the glass out of the water.
Turn it right side up.
Take out the paper.
Feel it.
The paper is dry.
The water did not touch it.

The paper was under the water.
You saw it.
But the paper did not get wet.
Let's find out why.

Push the paper into the bottom of the glass again.
Once more, turn the glass upside down.
Once more, push the glass all the way under the water.
Look through the water at the glass.
Water did not go into it.

But you can make water go in.
While the glass is under water, tip it a little bit.
A bubble of air goes out.

It goes straight to the top of the water.

When the air goes out, there is empty space
in the glass. Water rushes in.
You can see it. The blueing helps you see it.

Tip the glass more, and more.
One bubble goes out. Two bubbles go out.
Many bubbles of air go out.
Water goes in.

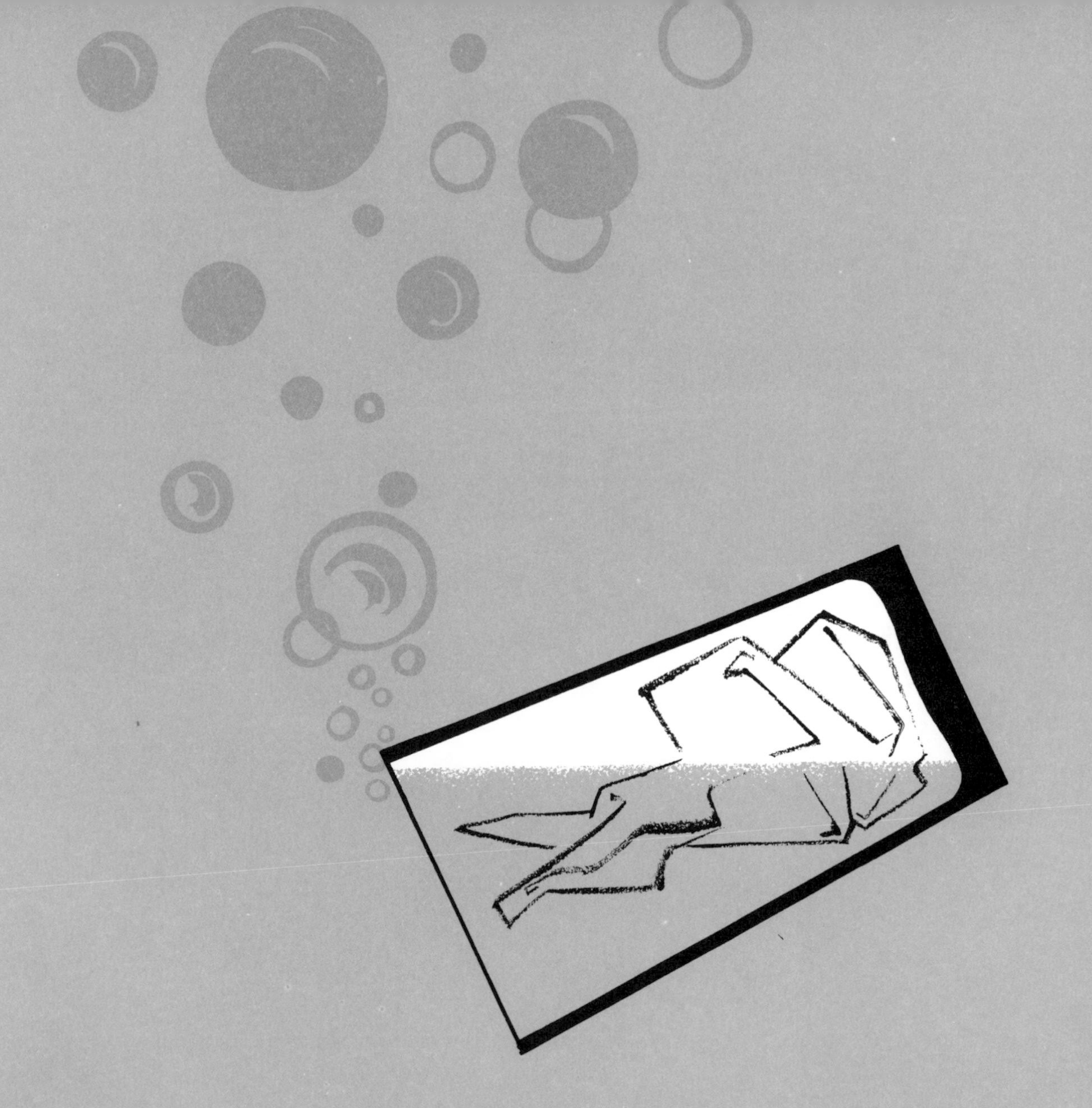

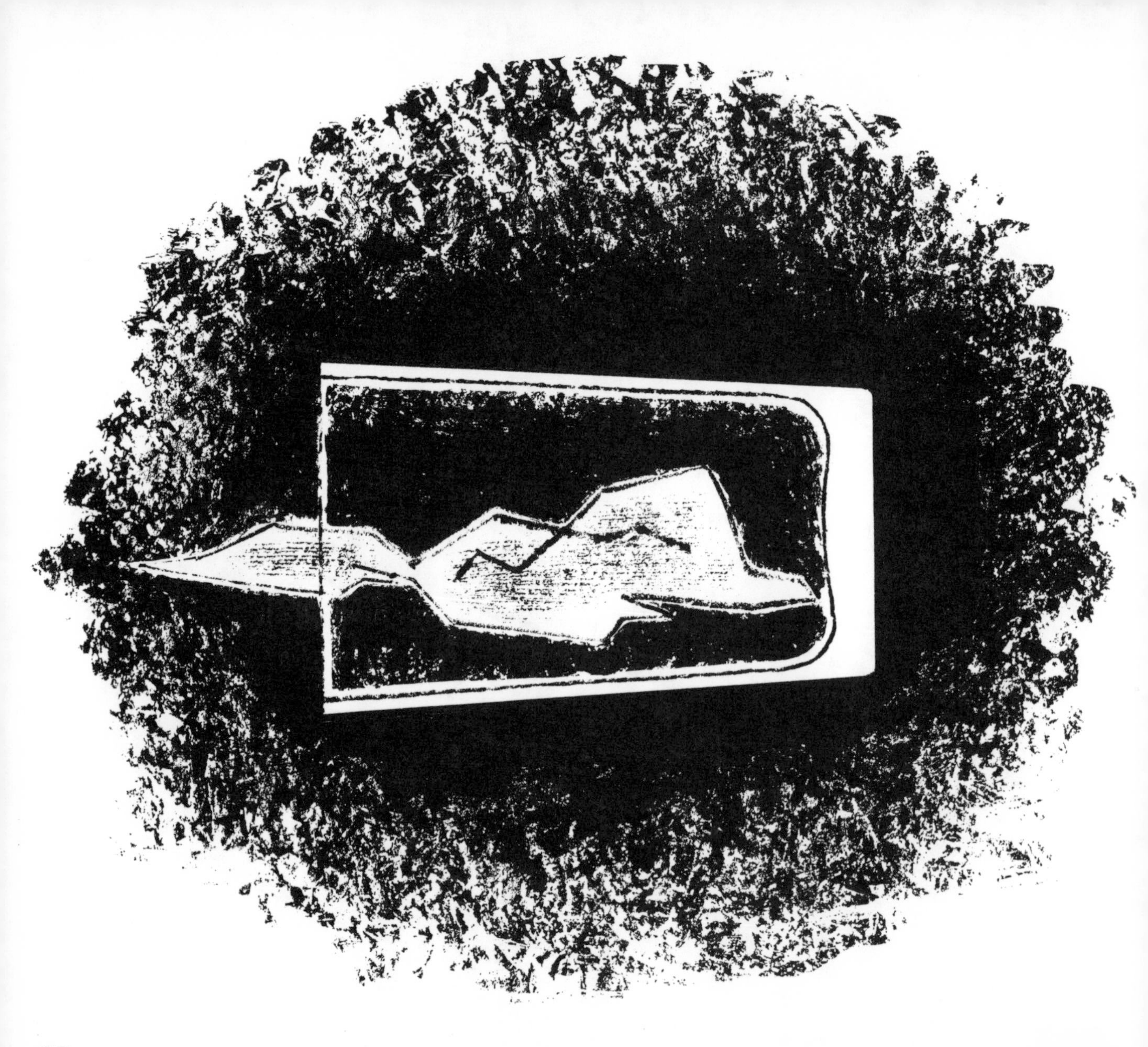

The glass is full of water.
The paper is soaking wet.

Air is in other things that look empty.

It is in a box.
It is in a car,
a tin can,
a pipe,
your dog's house.

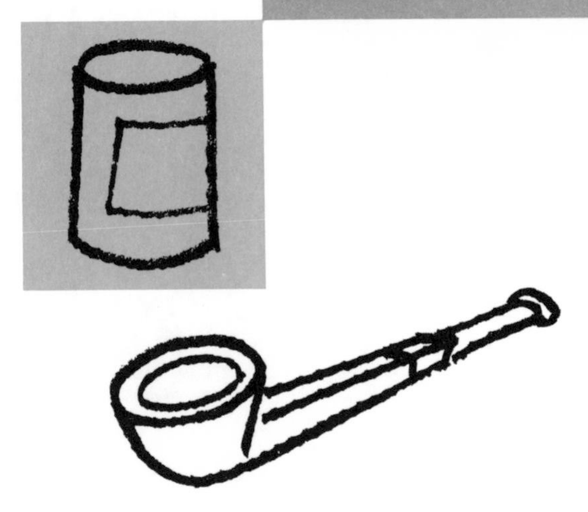

But air is not in everything.
Some foods are packed in tin cans.
The air is taken out of the can to keep the food fresh.

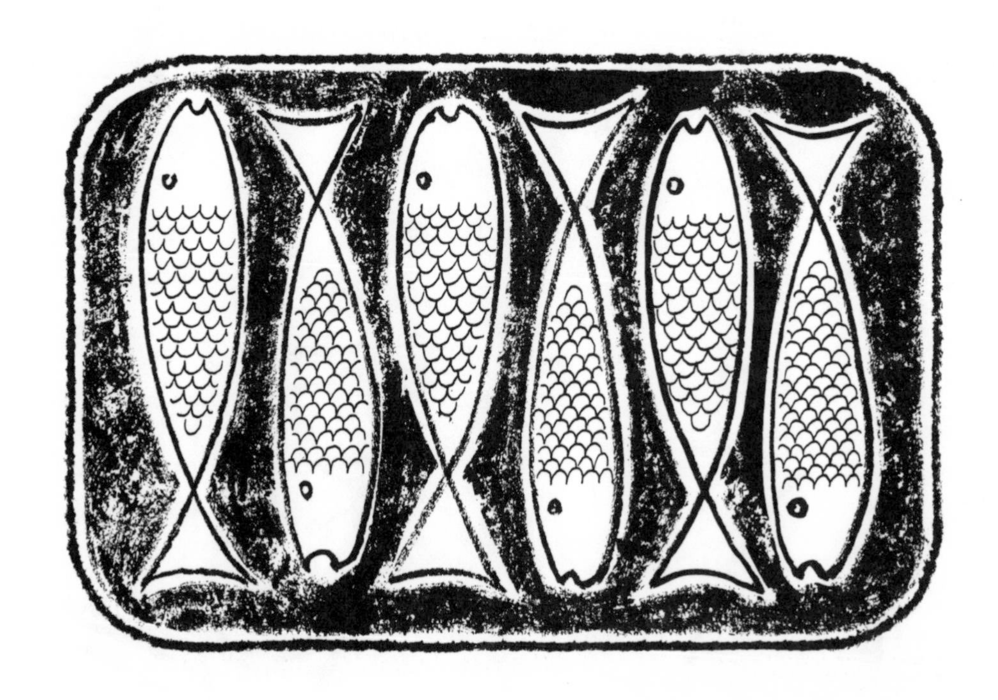

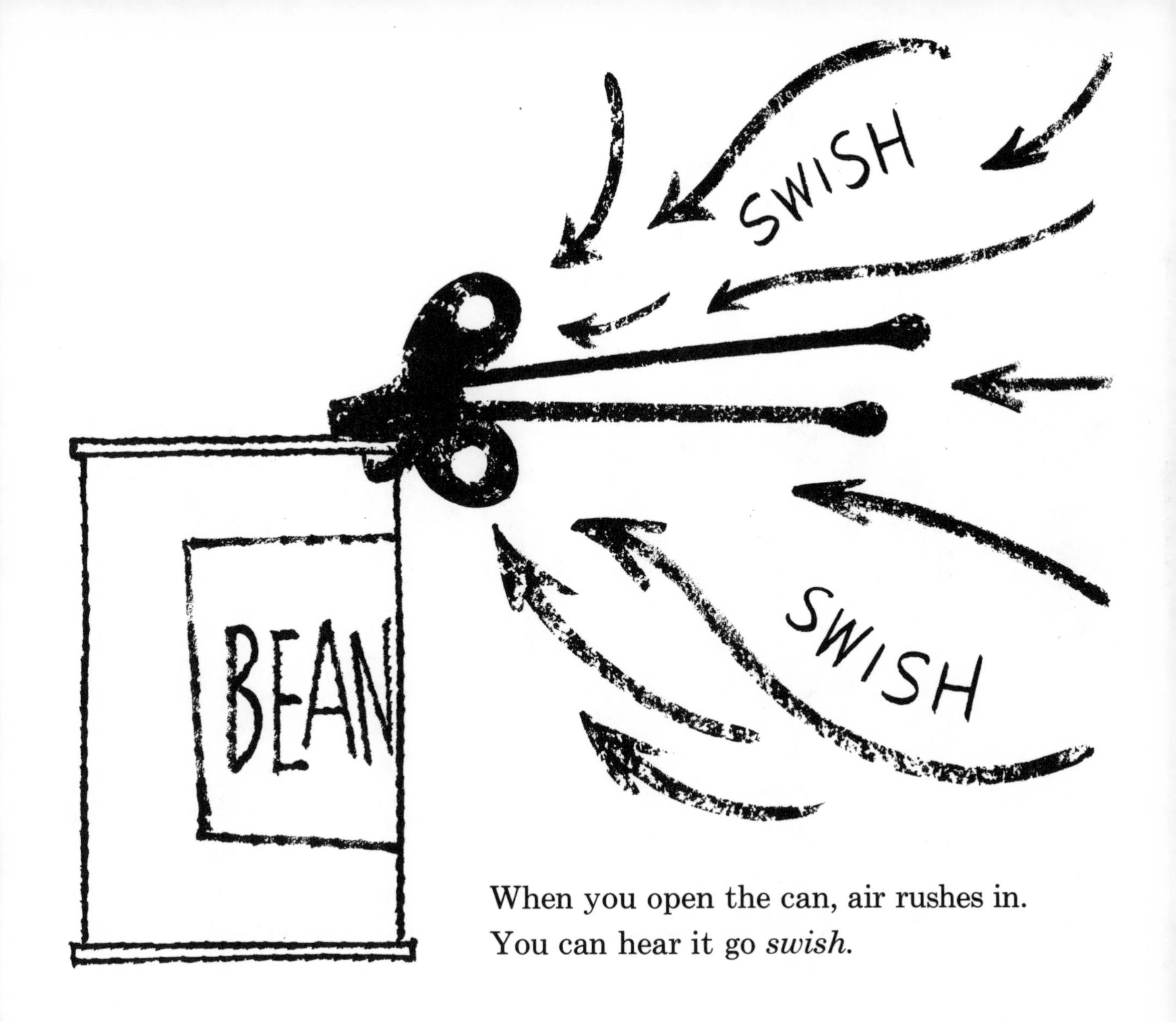

When you open the can, air rushes in.
You can hear it go *swish.*

But air is *almost* everywhere.
It is even in water.
That is hard to believe, but you can prove it.

Fill a glass with water. Look at it.

You cannot see anything in it.

In one hour, look at the glass again.

There will be little bubbles inside the glass.

The bubbles are air. The air came out of the water.

Air is all around you.
You cannot always feel the air,
but you know it is there.
Air is over you and under you.
It is all around you.

Wherever you go, whatever you do
here on earth,
AIR is all around you.

ABOUT THE AUTHOR

FRANKLYN M. BRANLEY is Astronomer and Chairman at the American Museum — Hayden Planetarium. For many years he has helped children learn scientific facts and principles at an early age without impairing their sense of wonder about the world they live in. Before coming to the Planetarium, Dr. Branley taught science at many grade levels, including the lower elementary grades, high school, college, and graduate school.

Dr. Branley received his training for teaching at the State Teachers College in New Paltz, New York, at New York University, and Columbia University. He lives with his wife and two daughters in Woodcliff Lake, New Jersey.

ABOUT THE ILLUSTRATOR

ROBERT GALSTER has illustrated many books for children. He has designed book jackets and record album covers and has painted murals for hotels in New York, Boston, and Florida. Mr. Galster is perhaps best known for his poster designs for the Broadway theater. He first became interested in poster design while he served with the Army Engineers in Europe. Mr. Galster is a native of the Illinois farm belt and grew up in Mansfield, Ohio. He now lives in New York City.